World Book's Human Body Works

The Skeletal System
The Muscular System

World Book, Inc.
a Scott Fetzer company
Chicago

World Book, Inc.
233 N. Michigan Ave.
Chicago, IL 60601 U.S.A.

For information about other World Book publications, visit our Web site at **http://www.worldbook.com** or call **1-800-WORLDBK (967-5325)**. For information about sales to schools and libraries, call **1-800-975-3250 (United States); 1-800-837-5365 (Canada)**.

World Book, Inc.
Editor in Chief: Paul A. Kobasa
Managing Editor: Maureen Mostyn Liebenson
Graphics and Design Manager: Sandra M. Dyrlund
Research Services Manager: Loranne K. Shields
Permissions Editor: Janet T. Peterson

Library of Congress Cataloging-in-Publication Data
The skeletal system/the muscular system.
   p. cm. -- (World Book's human body works)
Includes bibliographical references and index.
ISBN-13: 978-0-7166-4426-2
ISBN-10: 0-7166-4426-6
  1. Human skeleton--Juvenile literature. 2. Musculoskeletal system—Juvenile literature. I. World Book, Inc. II. Series.
QM101.S54 2007
611'.71--dc22
                    2006004689

World Book's Human Body Works (set)
ISBN 13: 978-0-7166-4425-5
ISBN 10: 0-7166-4425-8

Printed in China

06 07 08 09 10 5 4 3 2 1

Product development: Arcturus Publishing Limited
Writer: Andy Solway
Editor: Alex Woolf
Designer: Jane Hawkins

Acknowledgments
Corbis: cover, 4, 5 (Richard T. Nowitz), 19 (Robbie Jack), 33 (Lawrence Manning), 41 (Sears Wiebkin/Zefa), 43 (Ariel Skelley), 44 (Pete Saloutos).
Michael Courtney: 6, 9, 11, 12, 18, 24, 27, 31.
Miles Kelly Art Library: 30, 32, 36.
Science Photo Library: 7 (Dave Roberts), 8 (John Bavosi), 10 (Du Cane Medical Imaging Ltd.), 13 (Innerspace Imaging), 14 (BSIP/Dr. Amar), 15 (National Cancer Institute), 16, 17 (Anatomical Travelogue), 20, 21 (Helen Fournie, ISM), 22 (Dept. of Clinical Radiology, Salisbury District Hospital), 23 (Mehau Kulyk), 25 (Cristina Pedrazzini), 26 (John Bavosi), 28 (Michael Abbey), 29 (Steve Gschmeissner), 34 (Jason Kelvin), 35 (Ted Kinsman), 37 (Will and Deni McIntyre), 38 (Jerry Wachter), 39 (Leonard von Matt), 40 (NASA), 42 (Alfred Pasieka), 45 (David Munns).

Note: The content of this book does not constitute medical advice. Consult appropriate health-care professionals in matters of personal health, medical care, and fitness.

Features included in this book:

- **FAQs** Each spread contains an FAQ panel. FAQ stands for Frequently Asked Question. The panels contain answers to typical questions that relate to the topic of the spread.

- **Glossary** There is a glossary of terms on pages 46–47. Terms defined in the glossary are *italicized* on their first appearance on any spread.

- **Additional resources** Books for further reading and recommended Web sites are listed on page 47. Because of the nature of the Internet, some Web site addresses may have changed since publication. The publisher has no responsibility for any such changes nor for the content of cited resources.

Contents

Why do we move?

Human beings are always on the move in some way. Most of us can move our bodies on our own from one place to another. We can walk, run, jump, climb, and swim. We can use our hands to hold tools and make things. When we are not moving around or if an injury or disease stops us from moving, our ribs and chest are still in motion as we breathe, and our eyes blink. When we are standing, our bodies make tiny movements to stay balanced.

Inside our bodies, the heart is in motion all the time. From before we are born until the moment we die, the heart beats continuously.

On the move for food

Most people can get up and move about, but trees cannot. Why is this? The main reason is food. A tree does not need to move to get food. It can use water from the soil, gases from the air, and energy from the sun to make its own food. Humans and other animals cannot make food this way. We must move around to find our food. Even animals that move around very little or not at all, such as clams and barnacles, must move parts of their bodies to catch their food.

When we perform complex actions, such as climbing, muscles in many different parts of the body have to work smoothly together.

Different ways of moving

Spiders move around by using eight legs; insects use six. Cats, dogs, horses, and most other land *mammals* have four legs. Humans, however, walk on two legs. This lets our arms and hands remain free for such activities as using tools, lifting, and carrying.

So how do we move? What parts of the body give it its shape, and what parts enable it to move? How do we stay upright and keep our balance? How do bones form, and what do they do? How do muscles work? These are some of the questions this book will answer.

Even when we are asleep, some muscles are active. Muscles under the rib cage and between the ribs keep us breathing while we sleep. Other muscles push food through the gut as part of the digestion process.

FAQ

Q. Do we move when we are asleep?

A. Most people change their position several times as they sleep. While we are dreaming, our eyes move rapidly. Most people do not move as they dream. Some sleeping people do move as they dream, acting out what is happening in the dream. Sleepwalking is most common in children—about 1 in 10 walk in their sleep. Most sleepwalkers only sit up in bed, or stand next to it. But some do walk around, and they may even get dressed or eat something.

What gives the body its shape?

Before a body can move, it needs a framework, or structure, that arranges its parts so they can work. Our bodies are built on a framework called the skeleton. Most of the skeleton is made of strong, stiff bone. A few parts are made of a bluish-white rubbery *tissue* called *cartilage*.

The skeleton has about 300 separate parts when we are born, but as we get older, some bones join together, or fuse. An adult human has about 206 separate bones.

Support

The skeleton has many important functions. One is to support the body. Without the skeleton, our body would be a heap of tissue unable to do much at all. The bones of the feet and legs support the torso (the main part of the body). The legs both join to the *pelvis* (the hip bone) at the bottom of the torso. Rising out of the pelvis is the spine, or backbone, which is made up of bones called *vertebrae*. The spine supports the skull. The ribs, shoulders, and arms usually are not involved in support unless you are rolling, crawling, or doing a handstand.

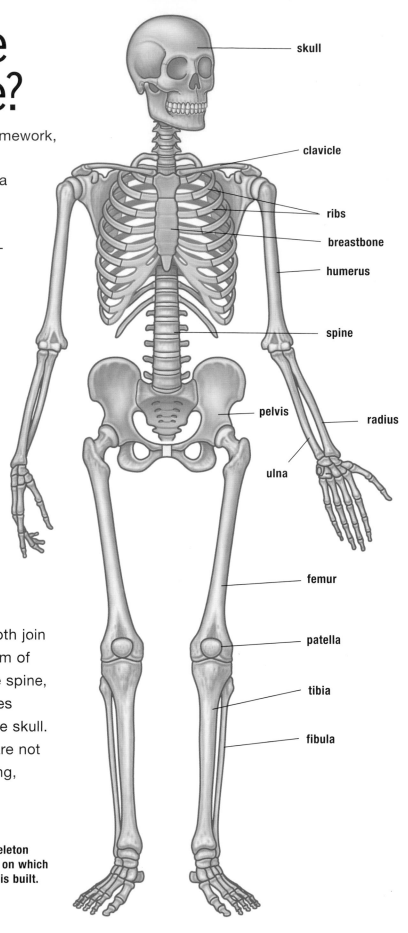

The bones of the skeleton form the framework on which the rest of the body is built.

skull
clavicle
ribs
breastbone
humerus
spine
pelvis
radius
ulna
femur
patella
tibia
fibula

Protection

A second main function of the skeleton is to protect some of the most important inner parts of the body. The parts that need the most protection are the brain and the spinal cord (the bundle of nerves running down the back). The brain is surrounded almost completely by the bones of the skull, whereas the spinal cord is protected by the vertebrae of the spine.

Motion

A third important job of the skeleton is to help the body move. The bones themselves cannot move the body, but muscles attached to the framework of the skeleton pull on the bones to make movements happen.

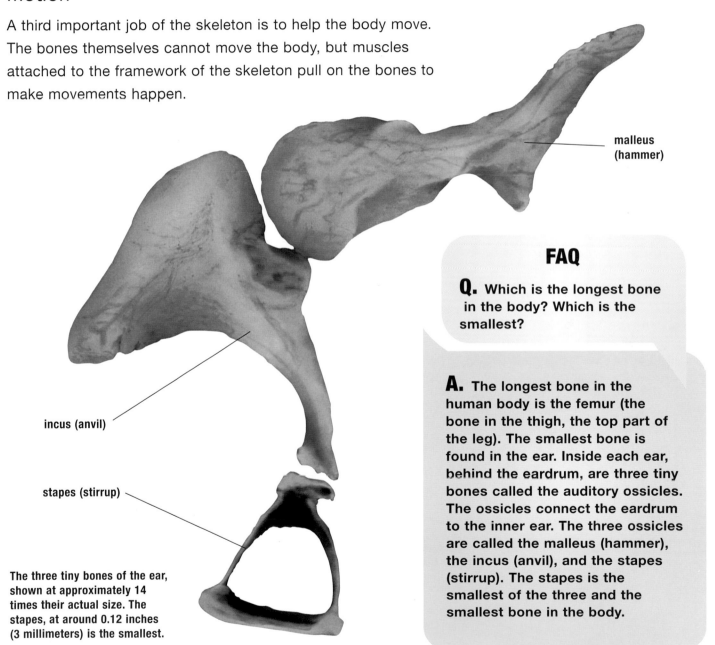

malleus
(hammer)

incus (anvil)

stapes (stirrup)

The three tiny bones of the ear, shown at approximately 14 times their actual size. The stapes, at around 0.12 inches (3 millimeters) is the smallest.

FAQ

Q. Which is the longest bone in the body? Which is the smallest?

A. The longest bone in the human body is the femur (the bone in the thigh, the top part of the leg). The smallest bone is found in the ear. Inside each ear, behind the eardrum, are three tiny bones called the auditory ossicles. The ossicles connect the eardrum to the inner ear. The three ossicles are called the malleus (hammer), the incus (anvil), and the stapes (stirrup). The stapes is the smallest of the three and the smallest bone in the body.

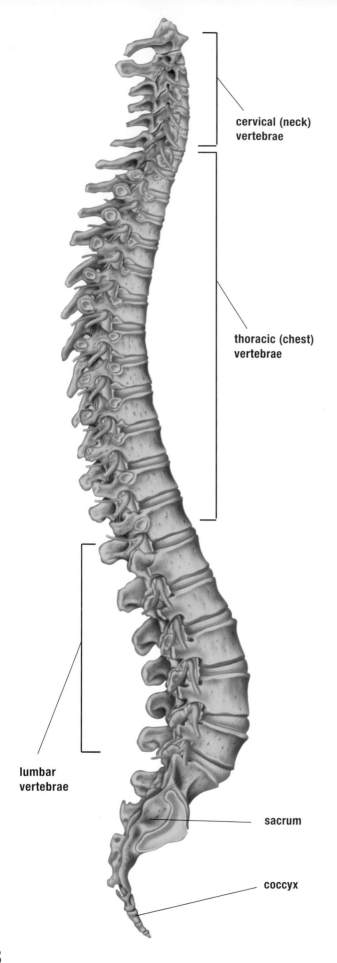

cervical (neck) vertebrae

thoracic (chest) vertebrae

lumbar vertebrae

sacrum

coccyx

Skull and backbone

The torso is structured around the spine, or backbone, with the skull balanced on the top end of the spine and the ribs curving forward from its upper section to form the chest.

An S-shaped spring

The human spine is a stack of 33 *vertebrae* that has roles in posture and movement and protects the spinal cord. The spinal cord is a rope of nerves connecting the brain with other body parts. Each vertebra has a large central hole that the spinal cord passes through. In adults there are 24 vertebrae, plus two bones at the bottom of the spine called the *sacrum* and the *coccyx*. In babies, the sacrum is made of five separate bones. These bones fuse together later in life. Three of the four coccyx bones in babies usually become fused in adults.

The spine is not a straight stack of bones. The stack curves in and out. These curves are very important for support and movement. They make the spine springy and able to absorb the shocks that travel up the legs every time you step or jump.

The ribs curve out from the upper section of the spine. At the front they join to the sternum (breastbone) to form the rib cage. This flexible cage of bone protects the heart and lungs.

The spine is made up of seven neck vertebrae, 12 chest vertebrae, and five lumbar vertebrae, plus the sacrum and the coccyx.

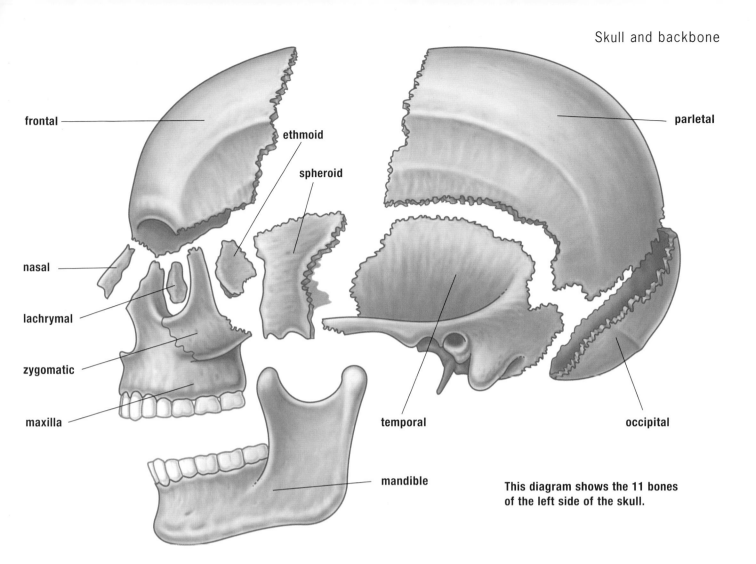

frontal

ethmoid

spheroid

parietal

nasal

lachrymal

zygomatic

maxilla

temporal

occipital

mandible

This diagram shows the 11 bones of the left side of the skull.

A bony case

The skull, which rests on the top vertebra of the spine, is made up of 22 separate bones. The main part of the skull is the cranium, or braincase, which protects the brain. The bones of the cranium are joined tightly together to make a strong casing around the brain. There is a hole called the foramen magnum at the base of the cranium, where the skull joins to the spine. The top of the spinal cord goes through this hole to connect to the brain.

The bones of the front part of the skull form the face and jaw. The muscles of the face attach to the facial bones. Only the top part of the nose is part of the skull. The rest of the nose is made of *cartilage* rather than bone.

FAQ

Q. Is a baby's skull the same as mine?

A. In adults the bones of the skull meet together tightly. However, in a baby the bones are separated by gaps called fontanelles. This gives the skull some flexibility. When the baby is being born, the fontanelles help the passage of the baby's head through its mother's birth canal.

Legs and arms

The legs and the arms have similar bones, but the legs are adapted for bearing weight, whereas the arms are adapted for freedom of movement.

The pelvis and legs

The *pelvis* consists of two hipbones, which are fastened strongly to the *sacrum* (the bone at the base of the spine). Together these bones form a bowl shape, which supports the organs of the *abdomen*. Each hipbone has a deep *socket* in it, where the top of the leg joins with the pelvis.

The bones of the pelvis, the sacrum, and the upper leg together form a very strong structure. The bones are held together by *ligaments*—straps of strong *tissue*.

The weight of the whole standing body rests finally on the feet. Each foot is made up of 26 separate bones. The bones of the foot form an arch, which spreads the body's weight across the foot.

An X-ray showing the bones of the foot. The central part of the foot has five long bones, each leading to a toe. The big toe has two bones, whereas the other toes have three bones.

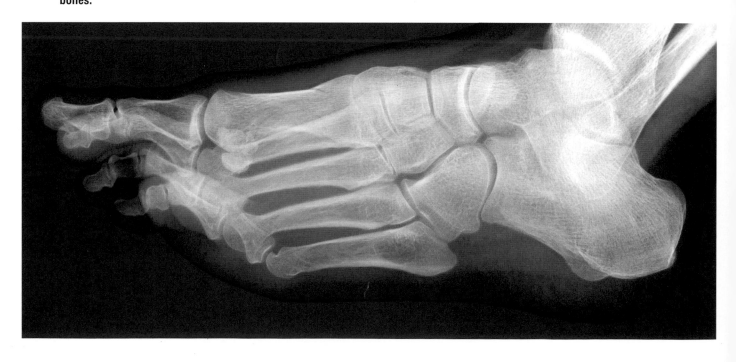

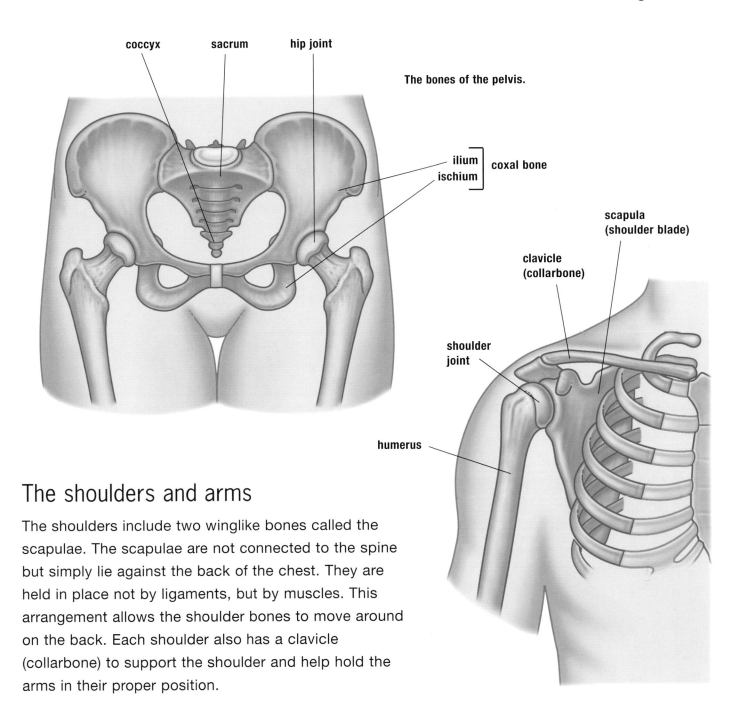

coccyx   sacrum   hip joint

The bones of the pelvis.

ilium ⎤ coxal bone
ischium ⎦

scapula
(shoulder blade)

clavicle
(collarbone)

shoulder
joint

humerus

The bones of the shoulder.

The shoulders and arms

The shoulders include two winglike bones called the scapulae. The scapulae are not connected to the spine but simply lie against the back of the chest. They are held in place not by ligaments, but by muscles. This arrangement allows the shoulder bones to move around on the back. Each shoulder also has a clavicle (collarbone) to support the shoulder and help hold the arms in their proper position.

On each scapula there is a shallow socket where the arm bone joins the shoulder. The shallow shoulder sockets give the arms a much wider range of movement than that of the legs.

The hands each contain 27 separate bones. The bones in the fingers are much longer than those in the toes, allowing the fingers to be used to hold things and do delicate work.

Inside a bone

The outside of a bone is hard, and the bone itself looks solid. But if you could look into a bone, you would see that the inside is made up of different parts.

What makes up bones?

The solid outer part of a bone is called compact bone. It is made from a hard material combined with the tough fibers of a *protein* called *collagen*. The hard material is made mostly of the *minerals* calcium and phosphate.

If the whole bone were made from compact bone, it would be heavy. Instead, under the outer compact layer, the bone is full of air spaces, similar to a sponge. This kind of bone is called spongy or cancellous bone. The long bones of the arms and legs have spongy bone at the ends, but the middle section of those bones is hollow.

The combination of hard bony material with hollow areas makes bones light but strong. Bone has a similar strength to wood. Bones seem stiff, but in fact they are quite springy. This gives the skeleton the ability to absorb impacts, such as those caused by running and jumping.

Living bone

The bones in your body are living things. Tiny living *cells* are all through the bones. Blood vessels bring food and *oxygen* to these cells, and nerves carry messages to and from them.

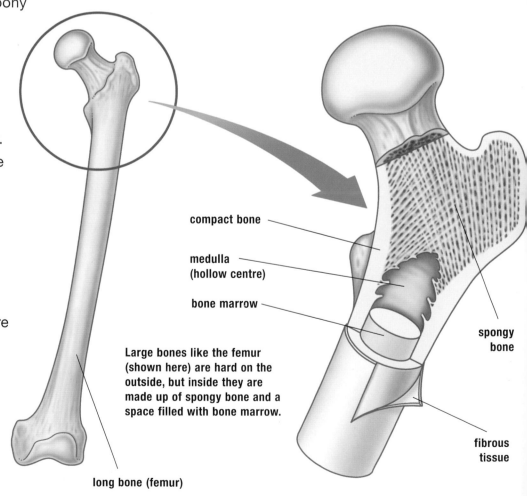

compact bone

medulla
(hollow centre)

bone marrow

spongy bone

fibrous tissue

Large bones like the femur (shown here) are hard on the outside, but inside they are made up of spongy bone and a space filled with bone marrow.

long bone (femur)

There are three main kinds of bone cell. Two of these, called osteoblasts and osteocytes, make new bone. The other type, called osteoclasts, break down bone material. Bones are constantly being broken down and remade. When we are growing, more bone is built up than is broken down. Once we are adults, bones are built up and broken down at about the same rate. In adults, bone is broken down and built up a small amount at a time, but even the small amount helps renew bone to keep it strong.

Other things can affect whether bones are broken down or built up. For example, if our diet is short of minerals, such as calcium, our bodies break down bone material and release the needed minerals into the blood. The minerals can be restored to the bones by eating a more balanced diet.

FAQ

Q. Does exercise affect your bones?

A. Regular exercise helps build up bones and make them stronger. Running or playing soccer, and other activities in which your legs bear your weight, are better for building those bones, for example, than such activities as cycling and swimming.

Compact bone photographed through a microscope. The black areas are canals through the bone that carry tiny blood vessels.

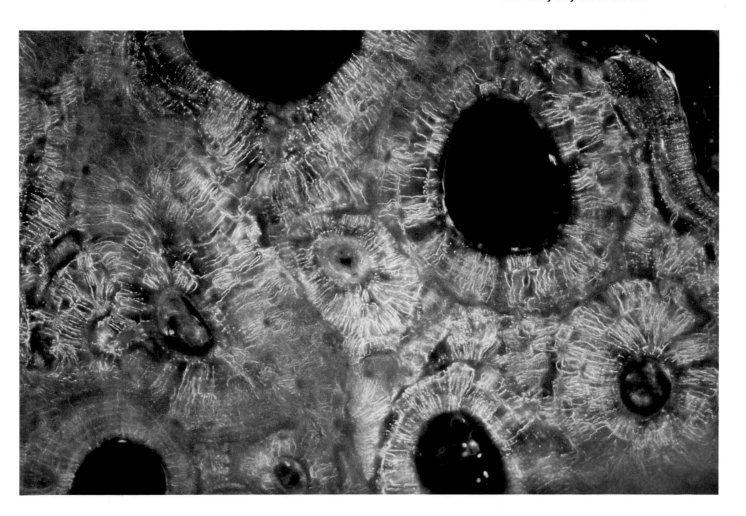

Blood and bone

In a living bone, the spaces and hollows are filled with a jellylike material called bone marrow. There are two kinds of bone marrow: red and yellow.

Red and yellow bone marrow

In babies and young children, all the spongy bone and the hollows of long bones are filled with red bone marrow. This kind of bone marrow produces blood *cells*. As people get older, red marrow in the hollows of the long bones is replaced by yellow bone marrow. Fat, a kind of nutrient that provides energy to the body, is stored in yellow marrow.

This microscope photo shows a megakaryocyte (center), with platelets developing on the surface (blue) and red blood cells (red) surrounding it.

Red bone marrow makes three different kinds of blood cell: *red blood cells*, *white blood cells*, and *platelets*. Most of the body's cells have a dark area called the *nucleus* inside them. White blood cells have this nucleus, but mature red blood cells and platelets do not. Red blood cells lose their

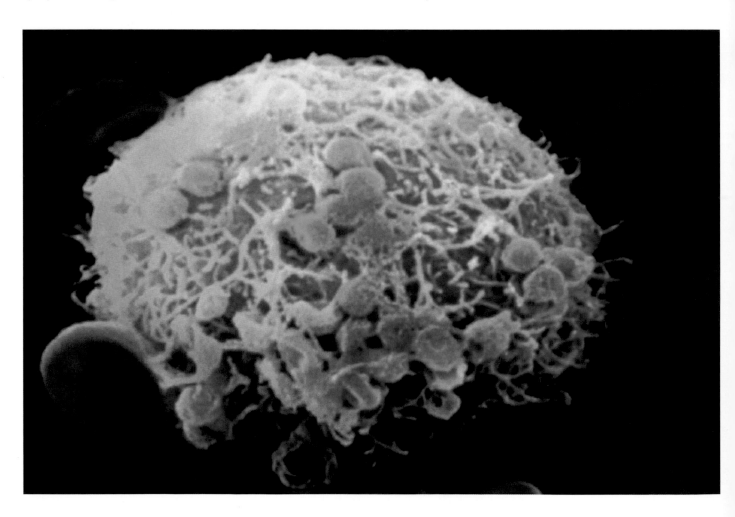

nucleus before they leave the bone marrow. Platelets develop from large cells in the bone marrow called megakaryocytes. Pieces of these giant cells break off to form platelets.

Billions of cells

The number of cells produced varies depending on the person and his or her age and health. However, a typical adult produces about 200 billion platelets and slightly more red blood cells every day. Every week the bone marrow produces enough red blood cells for just under a pint (about half a liter) of blood. The number of white blood cells produced varies greatly, depending on the person's health and the particular type of white blood cell. A healthy adult might produce up to 100 billion total white cells a day. While the person has an infection, his or her body would produce many more white cells.

A microscope photo of human blood, showing red blood cells (red), white blood cells (yellow), and platelets (pink).

FAQ

Q. What do the blood cells do?

A. One of the main jobs of the blood is to carry *oxygen* to all the body's cells. Oxygen combines with other chemicals in the cells to give cells the energy they need to function. Red blood cells contain a *protein* called *hemoglobin*, which carries the oxygen in the blood. White blood cells are an important part of the body's immune system (its defenses against disease). They destroy bacteria and other germs that cause illness. If you are injured and begin to bleed, then the blood platelets come into action. They play an important part in blood clotting.

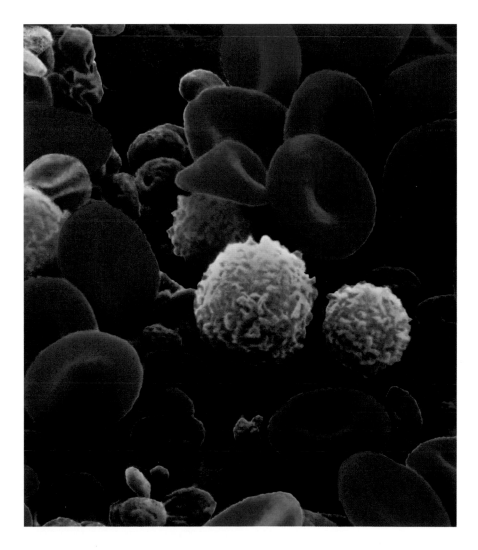

Changing bones

Bones change over time, but the greatest changes happen as you grow up. The skeleton begins to form while you are inside an organ in your mother's body called the womb. At first the skeleton is not made of bone at all; most of it is springy *cartilage*.

X-rays showing the hands of people aged (A) one, (B) three, (C) 13, and (D) 20. In X-rays A and B, there appear to be gaps between the bones. These gaps are made of cartilage.

From cartilage to bone

Your cartilage begins to turn into bone while you are still in the womb. Bone formation starts around the eighth week of pregnancy, the period in which you are developing in your mother's body. However, the process may not be complete until you are a teenager.

In most parts of the skeleton, bone forms from cartilage. However, the bones of the top part of the skull form directly from soft *connective tissue* (stringlike material that connects and supports internal organs).

Growing bones

As your body develops, some bones grow more than others. Of all your bones, the long bones of your arms and legs grow the most. Near each end of a growing bone there is a plate-shaped area of actively growing *cells* called the epiphysis. Cartilage forms on the inner side

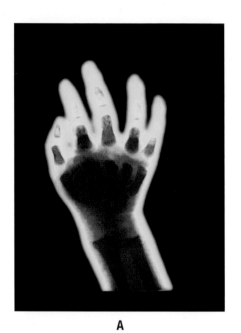

A

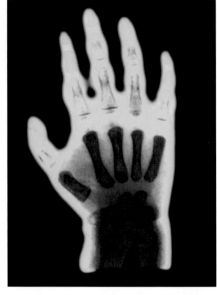

B

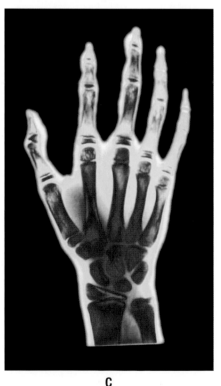

C

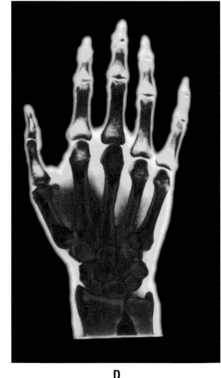

D

FAQ

Q. What is osteoporosis?

A. As people become elderly, their bones can become porous (full of small holes) and fragile. This bone disorder is called *osteoporosis*. If someone has osteoporosis, his or her bones can break easily and be slow to heal. People who exercise regularly when they are younger are less likely to get osteoporosis when they are old. Women are four times more likely to develop osteoporosis than men.

of this plate, then hardens and turns into bone. As new layers of bone are laid down, they make the bone longer. The epiphyses continue laying down new bone until you are fully grown and have reached your adult height.

As bones grow longer, they also grow thicker. New layers of cartilage and then bone are laid down by a layer of stringlike *tissue* that covers the outside of the bones. This layer is called the periosteum.

Problems in bone growth

Bones are often affected by a poor diet. If a child is not getting enough calcium, phosphate, or vitamin D in his or her diet, the child's body makes up the loss by breaking down bone tissue. As a result, the bones soften and can become bent or misshapen, and lumps may develop in the bones. Children with this condition are said to have rickets.

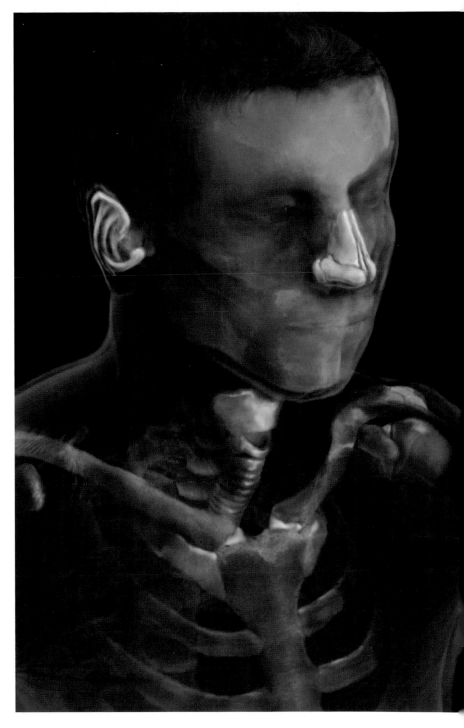

Even in adults, some parts of the skeleton are cartilage. In this picture, areas of cartilage are shown in white.

Connected bones

A place where two or more bones meet is called a joint. Some joints keep the bones fixed in one position, but most joints allow bones to move against each other, letting you move parts of your body.

Fixed joints

The joints between the bones of the skull are fixed—the bones cannot move against each other. The bones are joined to each other by stringlike *tissue*. This allows just enough flexibility in the joints to help protect the bones from breaking if they are bumped.

The joint between the two front parts of the *pelvis* (the pubic symphysis) allows a little more movement than the joints between the skull bones. The movement helps cushion the shocks that pass through the skeleton when we run and jump. When a woman gives birth to a baby, the joint becomes looser, to make space for the baby to pass through the birth canal.

Movable joints

Most of the other joints in the skeleton are movable. There are several different kinds of movable joint, which move in different ways. Hinge joints, such as those in the fingers, can only open and close in one direction, like the hinge on a door. In a pivot joint one bone can rotate in relation to another.

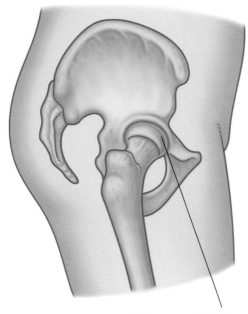

ball-and-socket joint

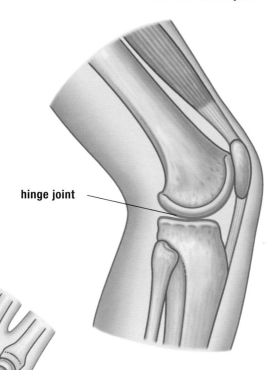

hinge joint

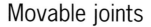

sliding joint
(carpal bones)

Here are three different kinds of joint. The hip is a ball-and-socket joint; the knee is a hinge joint; and in the wrist, several bones slide over each other to allow a range of movements.

The connection between the radius bone in the lower arm and the humerus in the upper arm is a pivot joint.

A third kind of joint is the ball-and-socket joint. In this type of joint, one bone has a ball-shaped end that fits into a cup, or *socket*, on the other bone. The ball can rotate inside the cup, allowing more freedom of movement than either a hinge or a pivot joint. The hip and shoulder joints are both ball-and-socket joints.

Synovial joints

Most joints are synovial joints. In synovial joints there is a layer of *cartilage* over the end of each bone so that their meeting surfaces move smoothly against each other. In the joint is an oily liquid called synovial fluid, which lubricates the joint.

FAQ

Q. **What does double-jointed mean?**

A. **People who are double-jointed have very flexible bodies. This is because the *ligaments* holding their joints together are looser than in most people. Double-jointed people should be careful, though, because extreme bending of the joints can cause joint problems later in life.**

The women in this circus act have extremely flexible joints.

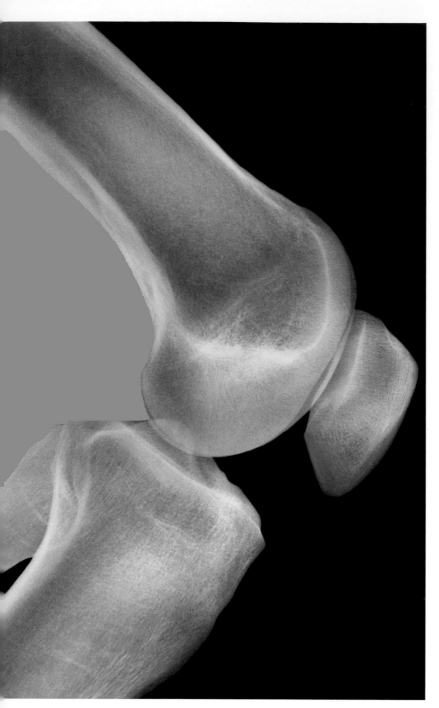

More about joints

Some joints in the body are not as simple as two bones meeting and moving against each other. The knee, for instance, is a complicated hinge joint between the tibia of the lower leg and the femur of the upper leg. Springy pads of *cartilage* cushion the connection between the two bones. At the front of the knee, a plate of bone called the patella (kneecap) stops the joint from bending too far forward.

Sliding bones

Probably the most complicated joint in the body is the wrist. There are eight bones (the carpals) connecting the hand to the forearm (the lower arm), arranged roughly in two rows. Three of the carpals form a joint with the radius, and the radius forms another joint with the ulna. The radius and the ulna are the two bones of the forearm. The joint made by the radius and the ulna allows the wrist to rotate so you can turn the palm of your hand up and down. The other carpal bones can slide over each other to give the wrist freedom to move in other directions.

An X-ray showing the bones of the knee joint. The patella (kneecap) protects the front of the knee and stops it from bending backwards.

Cushioned joints

The spine is jointed all the way down its length. Most of the vertebrae are separated from each other by cushioned joints. The front part of each *vertebra* is a rounded bony area called the body. The body of one vertebra is separated from the next by a cushion of cartilage called a disk. The outer layer of the disk is tough, but the inside is jellylike.

At the back of each vertebra, behind the hole through which the spinal cord passes, are two more joints. The combination of these joints with the large cushioned joint at the front gives each pair of vertebrae some movement forward, backward, and from side to side. Each pair of vertebrae can move only slightly, but taken as a whole, the spine is flexible and can move in many different ways.

FAQ

Q. Do people become shorter during the day?

A. Every day your spine shrinks by about one-half inch (1.25 centimeters), and at night it expands again. This happens because during the day you spend most of your time upright. The weight of the body pressing down on the disks between the vertebrae gradually compresses (squashes) them over the course of the day. As you sleep and the weight of the body is off the disks, they plump up again so that in the morning you are taller.

This diagram shows the joints between several vertebrae and the spinal cord.

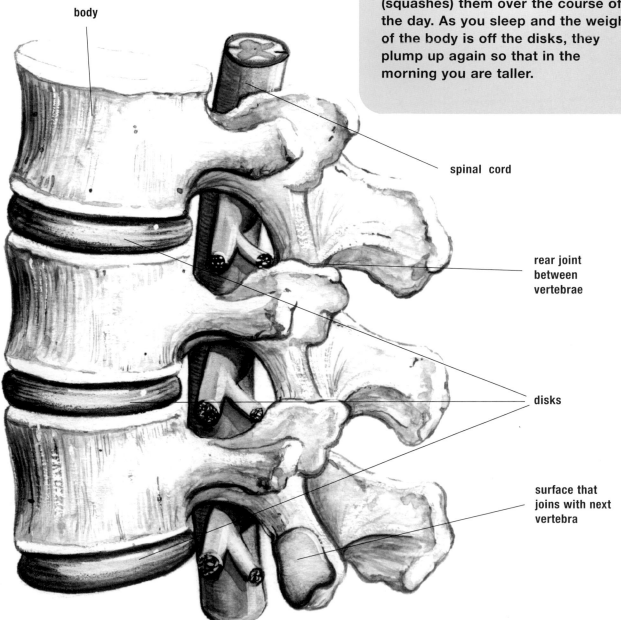

body

spinal cord

rear joint between vertebrae

disks

surface that joins with next vertebra

Damage and repair

Bones suffer wear and tear during a lifetime. Joints can be twisted, or sprained, and bones can be broken in a bad fall or other accident. But because bones are living *tissue*, they can repair themselves.

Fractured bones

The breaking or splintering of a bone is called a *fracture*. Almost as soon as a bone is fractured, it begins to heal. *Cells* move into the area around the fracture and build a stringlike bridge connecting the broken ends of the bone. Once a connection has been made, *minerals* build up in the bridge to harden it into bone. The healing process usually takes several weeks in young people, but fractured bones in older people mend more slowly. In adults the process may take months.

Helping bones to join

This X-ray shows that the bones of the lower arm (the radius and ulna) are both broken.

If a fracture is left to heal on its own, the bone is likely to set, or heal, crookedly. Doctors try to avoid this by stabilizing, or keeping motionless against each other, the parts of the broken bone. Putting a cast of plaster

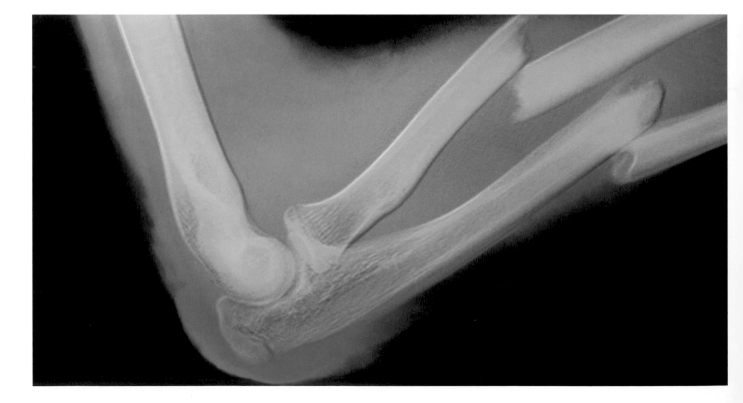

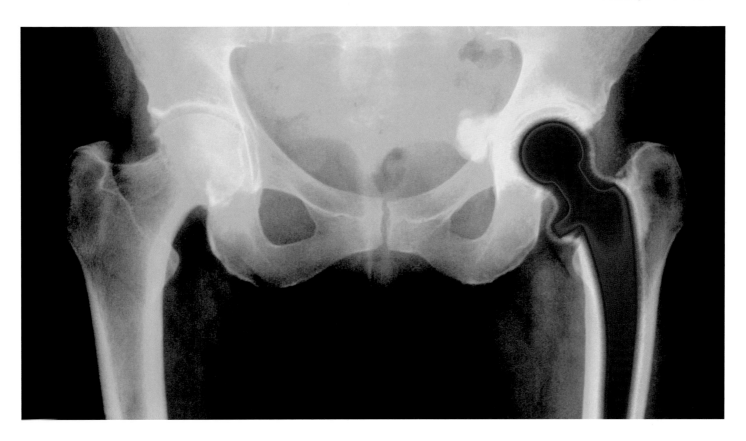

or other rigid material around the break will usually hold a fracture in place. Doctors also may use screws, metal plates, wires, or other devices to fasten the bone pieces together.

Damage in old age

In old age, bones become weaker and less flexible, and they break more easily. Many old people also suffer from a joint disorder called *osteoarthritis*. In this condition the *cartilage* covering the ends of bones meeting in joints begins to break down. At first the cartilage simply may be rough, causing some stiffness in the joint. But eventually the cartilage wears away, leaving the bones rubbing against each other. Joints can become very painful and may lose motion completely.

Osteoarthritis particularly affects hip and knee joints. In some cases doctors can treat osteoarthritis of the hip by replacing the joints. In hip replacement, a new joint is made out of metal, plastic, or porcelain.

An X-ray showing an artificial hip joint (pink). The head of the femur has been completely replaced.

FAQ

Q. How do surgeons mend badly damaged bones?

A. Sometimes a large piece of bone is too damaged to be repaired, or infection may keep a damaged bone from healing properly. When this happens, surgeons replace the damaged or infected bone with small chips of bone taken from elsewhere in the person's body. The chips promote new bone to grow in place of the removed bone.

Turning energy into action

The skeleton provides a framework for the body. The muscles are the parts of the body that enable it to move. A thick layer of muscles covers the skeleton and organs of the body. Some organs of the body are made of muscle.

What do muscles do?

Muscles do many jobs in the body. You need muscles to walk, run, lift and carry, hold things, write, draw, smile, and make all the other movements of your body. You also need muscles to chew and swallow food and to move the food through your *digestive system*. You use muscles to breathe, to talk, and to sing. The heart has muscles that pump blood throughout the body.

Although muscles working with other body parts help do many different jobs, each individual muscle can do only two things: it can contract, or tighten, and it can relax. When a muscle contracts, it gets shorter. When it relaxes, it returns to its resting length.

Doing work

When muscles contract, they are doing work, and work needs energy. The energy comes from the food you eat. Muscles turn this energy into movement.

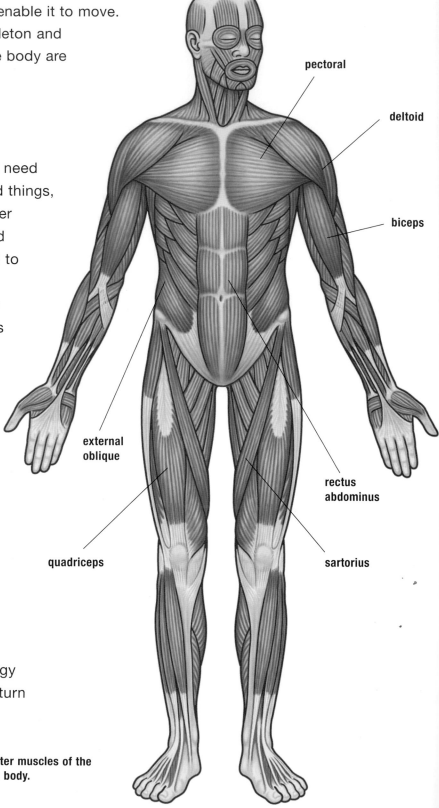

pectoral

deltoid

biceps

external oblique

rectus abdominus

quadriceps

sartorius

The outer muscles of the human body.

Try lifting your arm and holding it out at shoulder height. Before long your shoulder muscles will start to ache—they are certainly working! Muscles in the shoulder and arm contract to lift the arm up and hold it there.

Now relax your arm. What a relief! The shoulder muscles lengthen and the arm drops. No muscles have to work to make your arm drop—gravity does the job for you. And once the arm is by your side, no muscles have to work to keep it there.

This example shows that muscles work when they contract but not when they relax. This means that muscles can pull, but they cannot push.

FAQ

Q. **How many muscles do you have?**

A. **There are more than 600 muscles in the body. When you walk, you are using over 200 muscles. Your facial expressions are controlled by about 20 key muscles.**

Weightlifters, athletes, and other people who do hard, physical work develop large, strong muscles.

How do muscles work?

Muscles are made up of many bundles of long, thin fibers. The long fibers that make up these bundles are single muscle *cells*.

Blood vessels and nerves run between the fiber bundles. The blood vessels bring nutrients and *oxygen*—the fuel that keeps the muscles going. The nerves carry messages between the brain and the muscles.

How do muscles contract?

Each muscle cell is packed with long fibers of *protein*. The fibers are arranged in groups called myofilaments. The myofilaments contain two kinds of fiber—thick fibers and thin ones. The thick fibers are made mostly of the protein myosin, whereas the thin ones are mostly another protein called actin.

Bundles of actin and myosin fibers alternate along the length of the myofilament. The ends of the actin and myosin bundles overlap and are held together by small projections on the myofilaments. These projections are called cross-bridges.

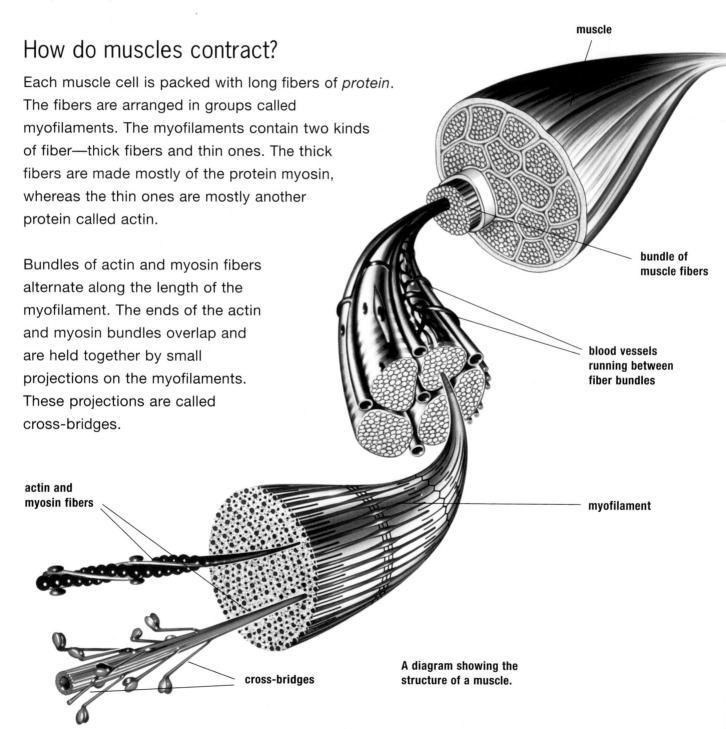

muscle

bundle of muscle fibers

blood vessels running between fiber bundles

myofilament

actin and myosin fibers

cross-bridges

A diagram showing the structure of a muscle.

When a muscle contracts, the actin fibers slide in among the myosin fibers. The cross-bridges between the fibers break and re-form, like someone climbing hand over hand up a ladder. The overall effect of the sliding fiber bundles is that the myofilament gets shorter.

Energy for contraction

It takes energy for the actin fibers to slide in among the myosin fibers. This energy comes from a chemical found in all cells. The chemical is called *ATP* (adenosine triphosphate). Cells make ATP using the nutrients and oxygen they get from the blood. When ATP breaks down to form ADP (adenosine diphosphate), it produces energy. The cell can use this energy to do work.

What causes muscles to contract?

Nerves stimulate muscles to contract. In resting muscle cells, two proteins called troponin and tropomysin stop cross-bridges from forming between actin and myosin fibers. Nerve signals sent to a muscle cause stores of calcium within the cells to bind with the troponin and tropomyosin. This frees actin and myosin fibers to form cross-bridges, making the muscle contract.

How a muscle contracts.

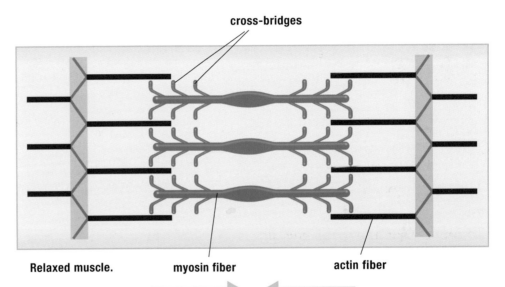

cross-bridges

Relaxed muscle.   myosin fiber   actin fiber

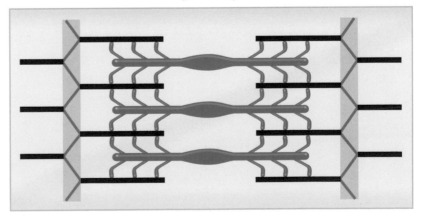

Contracted muscle.

Striped and smooth

There are different types of muscles in your body. The muscles that help you move your body are called *skeletal muscles*. They are attached to your skeleton and, in most instances, you can control them. Other muscles in the body contract and relax without you having to think about it.

Skeletal muscles

Most of the muscles in the body are skeletal muscles. They make up about 40 percent of the body weight of an adult male. Skeletal muscles are also called striated (striped) muscles because when seen through a microscope they have a striped appearance. The muscle fibers can be several inches (centimeters) long, and each one has many *nuclei*.

Smooth muscles

Smooth muscles are found in many places inside the body. Smooth muscles push food through the digestive tract. Smooth muscles also control the flow of blood through your blood vessels, and they are important in breathing and the birth process.

A microscope photograph of skeletal muscle.

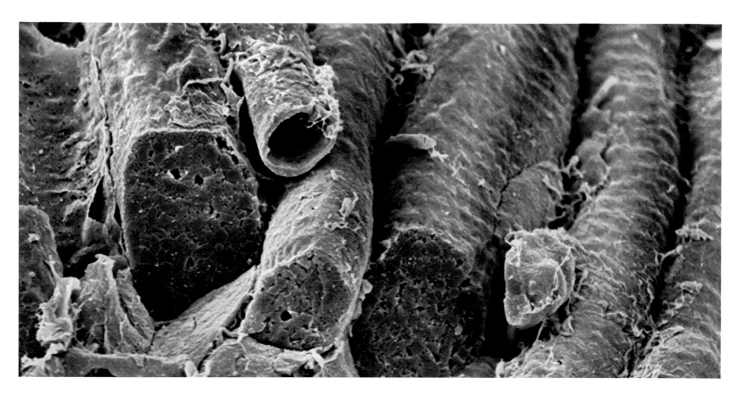

Smooth muscles do not look striped when seen through a microscope. These muscle cells are not as long as those of skeletal muscle, and they have only one nucleus. Smooth muscles do not contract as fast as skeletal muscles do, but they can continue to contract regularly for long periods without becoming tired.

A microscope photograph of smooth muscle, broken open to show the muscle fibres within. The red tube is a blood vessel.

Cardiac muscle

The walls of the heart are made of cardiac muscle. Cardiac muscle is like smooth muscle in some ways. The muscles are not under conscious control—the heart keeps beating even if you do not think about it. The cells of cardiac muscle have only one nucleus. Healthy cardiac muscles never tire. They can keep contracting in a regular rhythm for your whole life.

In other ways cardiac muscle is like skeletal muscle. Seen through a microscope cardiac muscle looks striped, and it can contract quickly like skeletal muscle. However, in cardiac muscle the myofilaments in each cell branch and join up with each other to make a network rather than bundles. This branching is found only in cardiac muscle.

FAQ

Q. How much does the heart beat?

A. Your heart is the most tireless muscle in the body. It beats in a regular pulse all your life, from before birth until death. Cardiac muscle may contract from 60 to 100 times each minute. In a lifetime of 70 years, this adds up to about $2\frac{1}{4}$ to $3\frac{1}{2}$ billion heartbeats.

Ligaments and tendons

Skeletal muscles need to connect to bones to be useful. Without its connections to the skeleton a muscle can do little more than twitch. Just as some joints are held together by straps of strong material called *ligaments* (see pages 10–11), muscles are connected to bones by strong cords known as *tendons*. Ligaments and tendons are made of similar material. They contain long, spindle-shaped *cells* called fibroblasts and bundles of *collagen* fibers.

Ligaments

Ligaments fasten bones together at the joints. The knee joint, for example, has four main ligaments holding it together. On the sides are two ligaments that keep the knee from moving too much from side to side. The other two ligaments run across an arch-shaped space between the two bones.

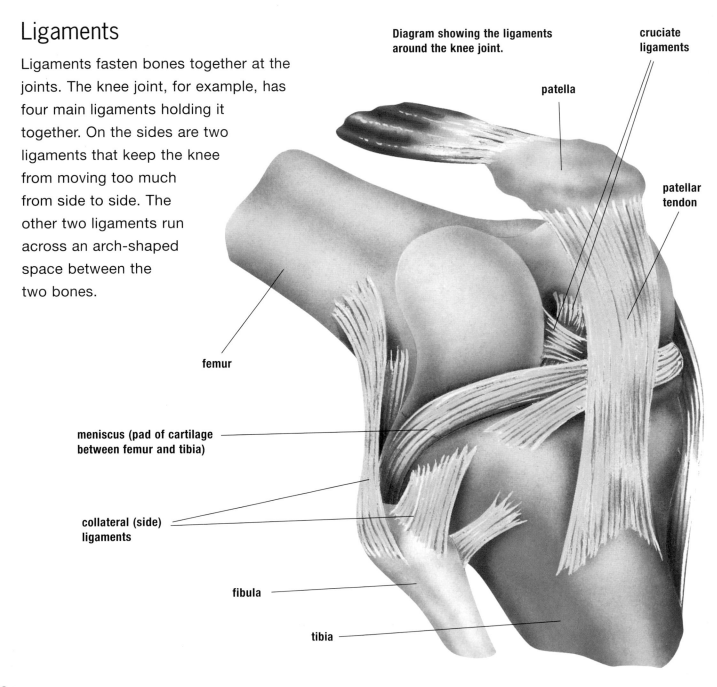

Diagram showing the ligaments around the knee joint.

cruciate ligaments

patella

patellar tendon

femur

meniscus (pad of cartilage between femur and tibia)

collateral (side) ligaments

fibula

tibia

One runs from the back of the femur to the front of the tibia, whereas the other runs from the front of the femur to the back of the tibia. The ligaments keep the tibia from sliding forward or backward.

Tendons

Tendons are similar to ligaments, but they connect muscles to bones or sometimes one muscle to another. The Achilles tendon, for instance, is the thick tendon you can feel at the back of your ankle, just above the heel bone. It connects the calf muscles to the back of the heel. When the calf muscles contract, the tendon pulls on the back of the heel and lifts it. This movement gives you the spring in your step when you are running, walking, or jumping.

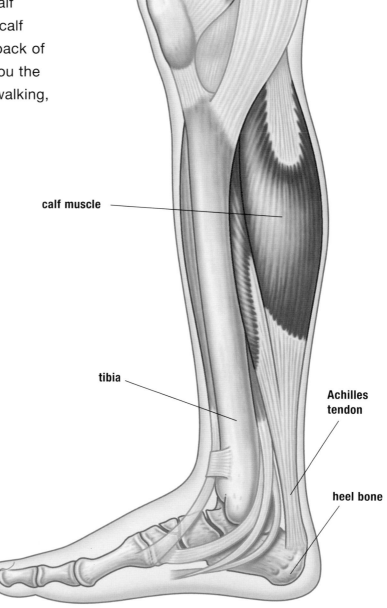

The Achilles tendon and its connection to the heel bone and calf muscles.

calf muscle

tibia

Achilles tendon

heel bone

FAQ

Q. What is a sprain?

A. A sprain is damage to the ligaments around a joint. Most often it happens when the joint is twisted or put under great stress. The most common types of sprain are to the ankle or wrist. A sprain is painful, and the injured part often swells up and turns black and blue. Doctors may prescribe rest, elevation of the injured part, or application of cold compresses to the injured part. An elastic bandage is often used to support the joint until its injured ligament heals.

Matching pairs

Muscles only can contract or relax. They can pull bones into a new position, but they cannot push them back again. For this reason, most muscles in the body work in pairs. One muscle contracts while the other muscle relaxes.

Antagonistic pairs

A pair of muscles that work in opposite directions is called an antagonistic pair. Antagonistic means conflicting or opposing. The biceps and triceps muscles in the upper arm are one antagonistic pair. The biceps is attached to the shoulder at one end and to the radius (main lower arm bone) at the other. When it contracts, the elbow bends. The triceps is attached to the humerus (upper arm bone) and shoulder at one end and to the ulna (smaller lower arm bone) at the other. When it contracts, the elbow straightens.

The action of the biceps and triceps muscles.

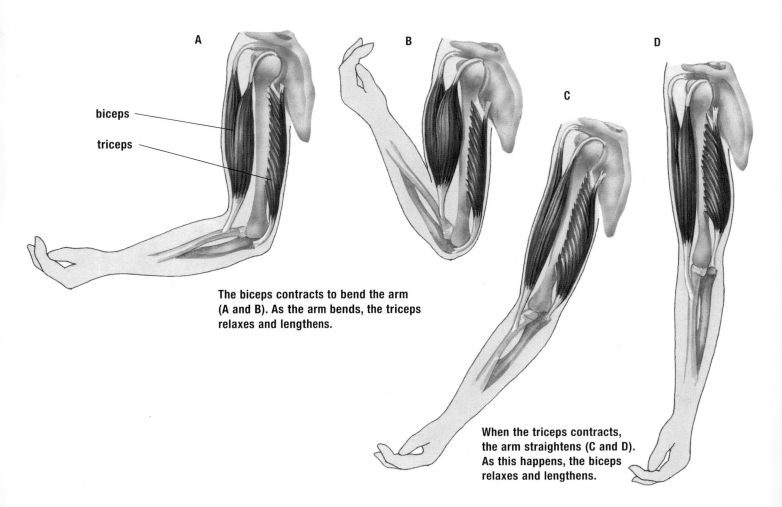

biceps

triceps

A

B

C

D

The biceps contracts to bend the arm (A and B). As the arm bends, the triceps relaxes and lengthens.

When the triceps contracts, the arm straightens (C and D). As this happens, the biceps relaxes and lengthens.

Flexing and extending

There are many other similar pairs of muscles in the body. One muscle of the pair is called a flexor because it flexes (bends) a joint. The biceps is the flexor for the elbow joint. The other muscle is called an extensor because it extends the joint. Some joints have more than one flexor or extensor. For example, there are three muscles for flexing the knee and three for extending it.

Twisting and turning

Many joints can do more than merely bend and straighten. For example, the upper arms and legs can rotate inward or outward. Two muscles in the chest are involved in rotating the upper arm. The muscle that rotates the arm inward is the upper part of the pectoral muscle—the large muscle you can feel on the front of your chest. The muscle that rotates the arm outward is called the deltoid muscle. If you put one hand on your opposite shoulder and then lift up the arm, you can feel the deltoid muscle.

When an athlete throws a discus, the whole body is twisted. Many muscles in the back and stomach are involved in this twisting action.

FAQ

Q. What are the biggest and smallest muscles in the body?

A. The biggest muscle in the body is the gluteus maximus—the main muscle in your bottom. The smallest muscle is the stapedius, a muscle inside the ear. It is about one twenty-fifth of an inch (1 millimeter) long.

We use any of 36 muscles to create our many facial expressions. The number of muscles used for each expression varies widely. Frowning uses far more muscles than does smiling.

FAQ

Q. Which muscle is the strongest?

A. That depends on what you mean by strongest. Of all the body's muscles, the cardiac muscles are the strongest in terms of endurance—they never stop working. The muscle that can exert the greatest force on an object relative to its size is the masseter, the muscle attached to your jawbone. But the muscle that has the most overall power to bear weight is the largest and thickest muscle of the body, the gluteus maximus (the muscle of your rump).

Other muscle jobs

Skeletal muscles do other jobs besides moving you around. You use your muscles to write, draw, and do other delicate work; to chew food; and to show your feelings through facial expressions. Muscles allow you to talk, sing, and breathe. And all your muscles generate heat as they work, which helps keep you warm.

Fine control

Humans are able to manipulate objects with their hands better than other animals. The main reason for this is the way we can move our thumbs. The muscles that move the thumb toward the fingers are well developed. This means that we can use the first finger and the thumb in opposition—we can press them together. Being able to move the thumb in opposition to the fingers is the main reason why humans can do so many things with their hands.

Central heating

The body has powerful muscles in the legs, back, and torso. Most of the power needed for standing, walking, running, jumping, and lifting comes from these muscles.

Because they are large and powerful, these muscles use a lot of fuel when they work. Some of this fuel gets turned into heat

energy rather than movement. Your body keeps warm by using the heat produced by your muscles that are working. One of the body's mechanisms for keeping itself warm in cold conditions is shivering. When you shiver, your muscles contract and relax very quickly, producing mostly heat.

This photo shows the heat that objects give off. Hotter areas show as red and cooler areas show as blue. The weightlifter is using his arm and chest muscles. Because they are working hard, these muscles are hotter than the rest of his body.

Making the air flow

Your body needs not only food for fuel, but *oxygen* from the air, too. Without oxygen, the muscles cannot turn nutrients from food into energy. To get the oxygen you need, you must breathe, and muscles play an important part in breathing. The main muscles involved in breathing are the diaphragm, which separates the chest from the *abdomen*, and the muscles between the ribs. When these muscles contract, they make the chest bigger and draw air into the lungs. When they relax, the elastic walls of the lungs push the air out again.

Reflexes

Our voluntary muscles are normally under our control. They receive instructions from the brain about when to contract. The instructions are sent along the nervous system. But if someone shines a light in your eyes, you blink and the pupils of your eyes get smaller without any conscious thought or effort. This is an example of a *reflex action*.

What is a reflex action?

Some reflex actions are responses to an emergency. The body uses reflex actions to get itself out of trouble. For example, if you touch by accident something hot, your hand will jerk away from it before you have a chance to think about it. Other reflex actions are fixed, that is, permanent or unchanging, patterns of movement. Stepping, for example, is a reflex action. Once you decide to take a step, the various actions that make up the step happen automatically.

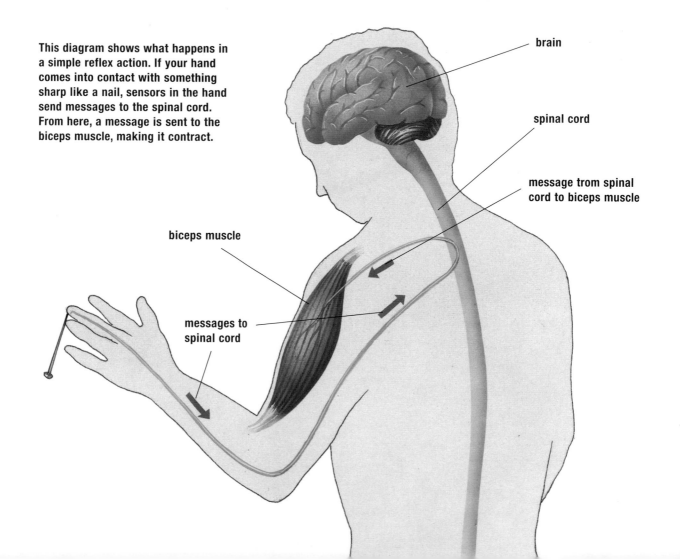

This diagram shows what happens in a simple reflex action. If your hand comes into contact with something sharp like a nail, sensors in the hand send messages to the spinal cord. From here, a message is sent to the biceps muscle, making it contract.

brain

spinal cord

message trom spinal cord to biceps muscle

biceps muscle

messages to spinal cord

The reflex arc

A reflex action is something that your body does automatically in response to a stimulus. It does not involve the conscious brain. In its simplest form, a reflex involves four things: a sensor, a nerve from the sensor to the spinal cord, another nerve from the spinal cord to a muscle, and a muscle. When the sensor is stimulated, it excites the nerve, which sends a signal to the spinal cord. There it meets with the outgoing nerve, which sends a signal to the muscle, and the muscle contracts.

FAQ

Q. Can we change reflex actions?

A. Reflex actions are not completely fixed. It is sometimes possible to consciously change your response. Coughing, for instance, is a reflex, but it is sometimes possible to stop yourself from coughing.

The knee-jerk reaction

Probably the simplest reflex action is the knee-jerk reaction. Doctors often test this reaction to see if a person's reflexes are working properly. The doctor taps the person's knee with a small hammer, making the quadriceps muscle in the upper leg stretch. Sensors in the muscle pick up this change and send a signal up a nerve to the spinal cord. The incoming nerve connects with two others. One sends a signal to the quadriceps muscle and makes it contract. The other sends a signal to the hamstring muscles in the back of the leg to keep them from contracting. The result is that the lower part of the leg kicks up as the quadriceps contracts.

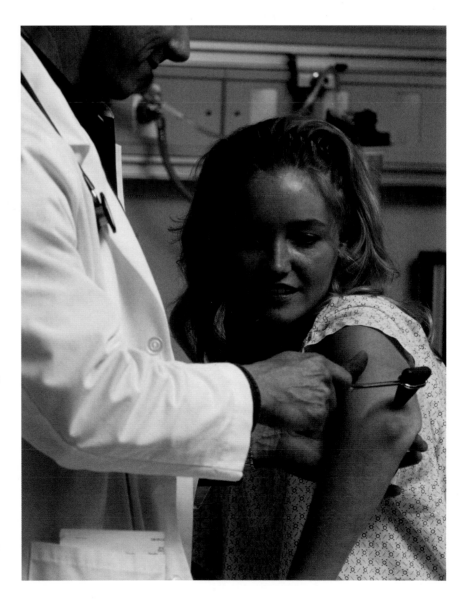

A doctor tests a patient's reflexes by tapping her elbow. If the sensors in her muscles are working, this should cause a reflex action: her lower arm should twitch as the arm muscles contract.

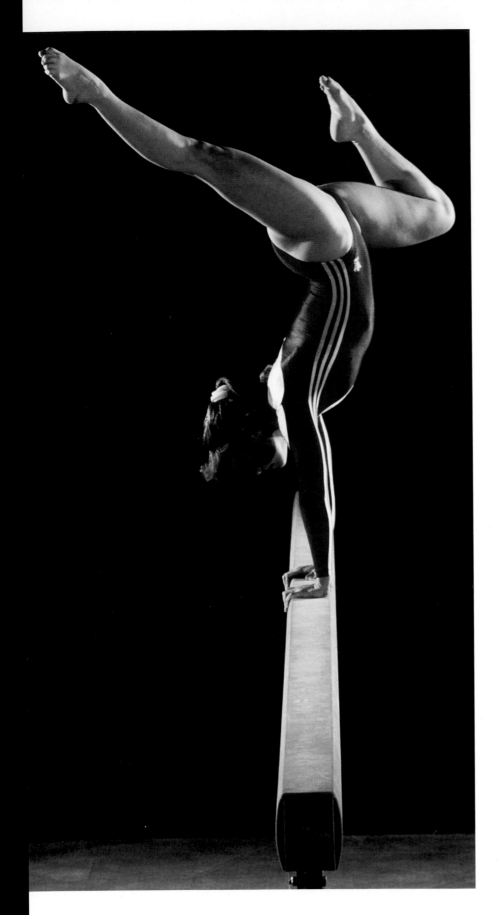

Balance and coordination

Your muscles are the engines that make you move, but without the brain and nervous system you would have no control over your movements. The brain plans your movements and sends instructions to the correct muscles to make movements happen.

Sensing movement

If you close your eyes and lift your arms, you can feel them move even though you can not see them. How do you know that your arms are moving?

You can feel your movements because there are sense organs inside your muscles, joints, and *tendons*. They send information to the brain that tells it whether a muscle is stretched or relaxed. These internal receptors are called *proprioceptors*.

Which way is up?

You get your sense of balance from an organ in the inner ear, inside the head. In the center of this organ is a chamber called the vestibule, which senses the orientation, or position, of the body.

The eyes give important feedback that helps the body to balance. A difficult exercise like this would be almost impossible with the eyes closed.

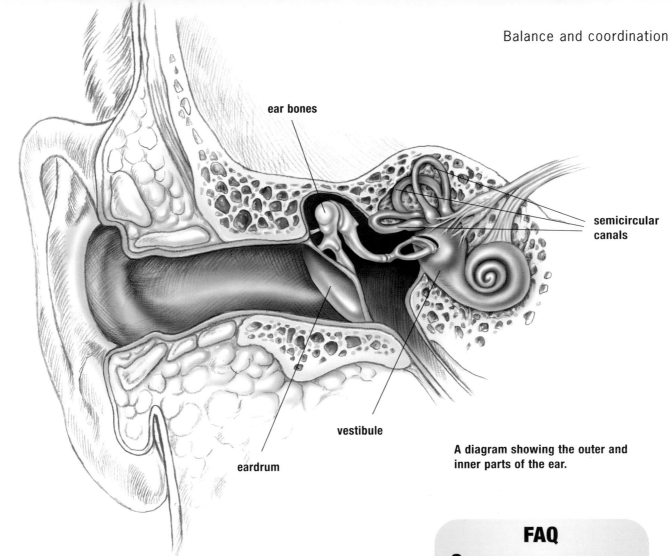

ear bones

semicircular
canals

vestibule

eardrum

A diagram showing the outer and
inner parts of the ear.

Around the vestibule are three curved tubes called the
semicircular canals. These three canals are at right angles
to each other, and they detect movement of the head in
any direction.

Coordination

The brain is in charge overall of your movements. When you
make any movement, the brain makes a plan of how the
movement will happen and sends messages to the muscles
that will make the movement. As the movement actually
takes place, the brain receives feedback from the balance
organs, the proprioceptors, and the other senses about the
progression of the movement. It uses this feedback to make
adjustments to the movement and keep it on track.

FAQ

Q. Can you make yourself
dizzy?

A. The semicircular canals in
your inner ear are filled with
liquid and contain tiny hairs
that bend when the liquid
moves. When you spin around
and then stop, the liquid in the
semicircular canals keeps
moving for a short time even
though your head is still. So the
balance organs tell the brain
that you are moving while the
rest of the senses tell the brain
you have stopped. The brain is
confused by the contradictory
information and you feel dizzy.

Exercise

When we exercise regularly, our muscles may grow bigger and stronger and they may tire less easily. Exercise also can help other parts of the body. The heart becomes stronger and pumps more blood throughout the body. And the lungs become bigger and take in more air.

Aerobic and anaerobic exercise

Your muscles need supplies of fuel and *oxygen* to keep working. If they cannot get enough of these supplies, the muscles are eventually unable to work. For short periods, however, your muscles can work without oxygen. This is called anaerobic exercise. The muscles get energy by breaking down the sugars they use as fuel. During anaerobic exercise, this process throws off a chemical called *lactic acid*. Later, when the muscles have finished working, they will use oxygen to break down and get rid of this lactic acid.

Muscles quickly become weak in the zero gravity of space, so astronauts must exercise regularly to keep the muscles working.

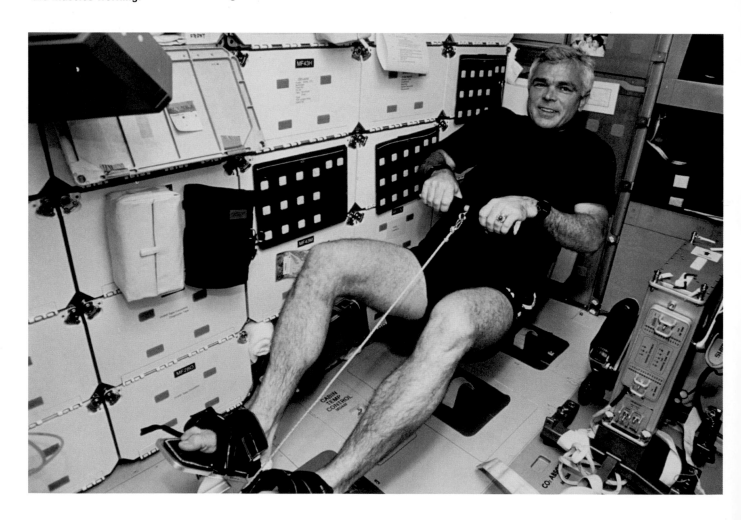

Muscles can work anaerobically only for a short time. If muscles continue to work hard without getting enough oxygen, lactic acid builds up in the muscles. When this happens, the muscles become tired and cannot contract well.

To exercise or work for longer periods, muscles need to function aerobically. In aerobic exercise the muscles work less hard and can get enough oxygen to contract. Lactic acid does not build up, and the muscles can keep working.

Different kinds of exercise

Different kinds of exercise produce different effects on the muscles and bones. Endurance exercises, such as running, swimming, and cycling, are aerobic. They can make the muscles stronger and less easily tired. Endurance exercises also can make the heart stronger and increase the capacity of the lungs.

For such sports as sprinting, athletes develop fast-twitch muscles and the ability to exercise anaerobically.

Such exercises as weight lifting and sprinting use the muscles anaerobically. The muscles quickly become bigger and more powerful. Anaerobic exercise can strengthen the bones. However, this kind of exercise has less effect on the heart and lungs.

FAQ

Q. Do sprinters and marathon runners develop different muscles?

A. There are two different kinds of muscle fibers in muscle. Slow-twitch muscle fibers contract slowly but keep going for a long time, whereas fast-twitch muscle fibers contract quickly but soon get tired. Sprinters develop lots of fast-twitch muscle fibers, whereas the muscles of marathon runners develop mostly slow-twitch fibers.

Slowing down

As people get older, they begin to move more slowly and their bodies become less able to grow and repair themselves. This is part of the natural process of aging. Aging can lead to problems with bones and muscles. However, people who exercise regularly throughout life are much less likely to have such problems.

Changes in bones

In older people, bones often become thin and brittle because they lose calcium and other *minerals*. As a result, bones are easily broken and slow to heal. Changes to the spine may occur in older people, too. The disks between the *vertebrae* may become thinner, and the spine become more curved. Joints can become stiff as the *cartilage* covering the bone ends wears away. In many cases the joints become inflamed (swell up) and are stiff and painful.

This computer simulation shows how the skeleton can change in old age.

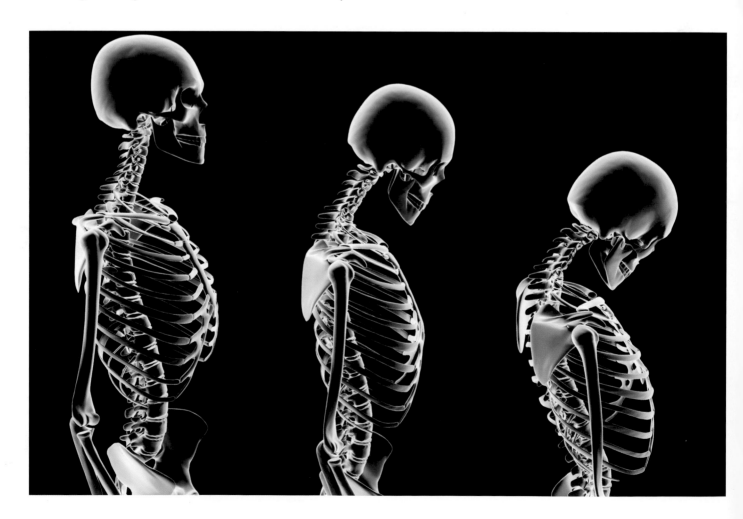

Changes in muscles

As we get older, our muscles begin to shrink and lose bulk. We also begin to lose muscle fibers, and muscles respond less quickly (they take longer to contract). The combination of stiff hands and weaker muscles mean that hands cannot grip so strongly, and it may become difficult for older people to do such things as opening jars or turning door knobs. Like the other muscles, the heart also becomes less strong with age.

Although people become weaker with age, their endurance often improves. Older athletes who are healthy may find that they actually do better in long-distance events than they did when they were younger.

People who exercise regularly throughout their life are more likely to remain strong and supple as they get older.

FAQ

Q. Can we slow down the effects of aging?

A. If you exercise regularly when you are younger, your muscles and bones likely would be thick and strong. So when you get older and begin to lose muscle and bone, it has less effect than on someone who has done little exercise. Continuing to exercise and stretch as you get older also can slow down losses of bone and muscle. Including plenty of calcium in your diet helps to keep bones strong and muscles working well (see page 45). Calcium is the most important mineral in bone *tissue*, and it also plays an important part in muscle contraction (see page 27).

Caring for bones and muscles

Most of the time we take moving for granted. We run up the stairs or throw a ball without really thinking about it. But you need to take care of your bones and muscles to make sure they continue to perform well throughout your life.

Exercise

Your body is designed for movement. Too much sitting around is not good for you. Regular exercise helps keep your muscles strong and healthy. Exercise also helps keep your bones strong. If your muscles became stronger but your bones were thin, the pull of a strong muscle could damage the bone. So the body builds up your bone strength as the muscles get stronger.

FAQs

Q. Why is good posture important?

A. How you stand and hold yourself is known as posture. Good posture helps your body's systems function properly. For good posture you need to stand tall and relaxed. One way to do this is to imagine a large balloon above your head gently pulling your whole body straight and tall. You can even imagine what color your balloon is. To improve your posture, just think *Balloon on!*

Cycling is one kind of exercise that helps develop strong muscles and bones.

Any activity in which you move around and use plenty of energy counts as exercise. You probably get plenty of exercise without even thinking about it. Maybe you walk to school regularly, do sports, or ride your bike. All these activities help to keep your bones and muscles in good working order.

Protection

Exercise is good for you, but it is important to exercise properly to avoid injuries. Warm up your muscles gently before doing a sport or any heavy exercise, for example by running in place, and do a series of stretches afterward. This will help keep muscles and *tendons* supple and avoid such injuries as sprains and torn muscles.

Eating a balanced diet is as important for keeping bones and muscles healthy as doing regular exercise.

Nutrition

Calcium forms an important part of bones (see page 12), and it is involved in making muscles contract (see page 27). Such dairy products as milk, cheese, and yogurt are rich in calcium. Eating plenty of these foods helps to build up bones and keep muscles working properly. Most adults should choose reduced-fat or fat-free dairy foods to help avoid health problems associated with fatty foods.

Glossary

abdomen The lower part of the torso; the stomach area.

ATP (adenosine triphosphate) A high-energy substance that cells can use to do work.

cartilage The springy but tough material that forms some parts of the skeleton and joints.

cell The basic building block of the body.

coccyx The bone at the bottom of the spine attached to the sacrum.

collagen A stringy kind of protein that forms an important part of bones, tendons, and ligaments.

connective tissue The strong, stringy material that connects and supports internal organs.

digestive system The stomach, intestines, and other parts of the body that break down food.

fracture A broken bone.

hemoglobin The substance in red blood cells that carries oxygen throughout the body.

lactic acid The waste material that builds up in the blood when the body is exercising anaerobically.

ligaments Straps of tissue that connect bones together.

mammal A warm-blooded animal that usually has a covering of hair or fur. Mammals feed their young milk from special mammary glands. Humans, dogs, horses, and mice are examples of mammals.

mineral A simple chemical that can be dug out of the ground or is found in the soil.

nucleus (plural: nuclei) The central part of a living cell, which contains the genes.

osteoarthritis A disorder in which the joints become stiff, swollen, and painful.

osteoporosis A disease that affects some older people in which the bones become fragile and do not easily heal when damaged.

oxygen A gas in the air that our bodies need in order to get energy from food.

pelvis The hip bones.

platelets Small fragments of cells found in the blood that are important for blood clotting.

proprioceptor A sense organ that detects stretching in the muscles.

protein A type of chemical in food that living things use for making some parts of the body and for speeding up the chemical reactions that happen in a cell.

red blood cell The type of cell that makes up about 40 percent of the blood and carries oxygen throughout the body.

reflex action An automatic response to a stimulus.

sacrum The bottom part of the spine that forms part of the pelvis.

skeletal muscle The type of muscle that moves you around (also called *striated muscle*).

smooth muscle A type of muscle that is not under conscious control and is found in the digestive system, the blood vessels, and other body organs.

socket A smooth hollow in a bone where another bone fits to form a joint.

tendon A cord that connects muscle to bone or to other muscle.

tissue A part of the body made from cells that are all similar. Muscles are one kind of tissue, and skin is another.

vertebra (plural: vertebrae) One of the bones that make up the spine.

white blood cell One of several kinds of larger blood cell that is important for defending the body against disease.

Additional resources

Books

Arnold, Nick. *(Horrible Science) Blood, Bones and Body Bits.* New York: Point Signature, 1998.

Ballard, Carol. *(Exploring the Human Body) The Skeleton and Muscles.* San Diego, CA: KidHaven Press, 2005.

Llewellyn, Claire. *The Big Book of Bones: An Introduction to Skeletons.* New York: Peter Bedrick Books, 2001.

Simon, Seymour. *Muscles: Our Muscular System.* New York: HarperTrophy, 2000.

Walker, Richard. Encyclopedia of the Human Body. New York: DK Publishing, 2002.

Wood, Lily. *(Scholastic Science Readers) Skeletons.* New York: Scholastic Reference, 2001.

Web sites

http://www.lumen.luc.edu/lumen/meded/grossanatomy/dissector/mml/
Master Muscle List. Choose any muscle in the body and find out what it does.

http://kidshealth.org/kid/
Information and games about keeping fit, eating well, sports injuries, and other topics.

http://www.bbc.co.uk/science/humanbody/
BBC Human Body and Mind. An interactive Web site about the muscles, skeleton, and other body systems.

Index